THE OFFICIAL
WEST HAM
1895 UNITED 2020
ANNUAL 2021

WRITTEN BY ROBIN JOHNSON
DESIGNED BY JODIE CLARK

CONTENTS

WELCOME TO THE OFFICIAL WEST HAM UNITED ANNUAL 2021!

125 YEARS TOGETHER

1895   2020

UNITED FOREVER

WEST HAM UNITED FOOTBALL CLUB

COMMEMORATIVE 125TH ANNIVERSARY

HOME KIT 2020/21

officialwesthamstore.com

THIS ANNUAL BELONGS TO...

George M

MY AGE:

9

MY BIRTHDAY:

Jan 3rd

MY COUNTRY:

ENGland

MY FOOTBALL TEAM:

west ham

MY POSITION:

Defence

MY FAVOURITE WEST HAM UNITED PLAYER:

Lucas pacuta

MY FAVOURITE PLAYER IN THE WORLD:

Sommaea

A PICTURE OF ME IN MY KIT:

I LOVE WEST HAM BECAUSE:

THERE THE BEST!!!!!

125 YEARS
OF WEST HAM UNITED:
TROPHIES!

West Ham United are now an absolutely massive 125 years old! Way back in June 1895, a group of friends at the Thames Ironworks and Shipbuilding Company, out in east London, decided to start their own football team.

Back then, West Ham United were known as 'Thames Ironworks FC', their stadium was called Hermit Road, there was no manager (the team was picked by a vote) – and their kits were completely blue!

Now 125 years later, dressed in our world-famous Claret and Blue, West Ham United have won some of the biggest trophies in football. Check out all our silverware below!

3 FA CUPS

West Ham have won the biggest cup competition in England THREE times: in 1964, 1975 and 1980! We also reached the final in 1923 and 2006.

1 EUROPEAN CUP WINNERS' CUP

The UEFA Cup Winners' Cup was a competition between all the teams in Europe who had won their biggest cups – and West Ham beat 1860 Munich 2-0 in the 1965 final!

1 UEFA INTERTOTO CUP

Our most recent big trophy came in August 1999, when we beat FC Metz 3-2, over two games, to qualify for the Europa League (then called the 'UEFA Cup')!

2 SECOND DIVISION PROMOTIONS

You might know this competition as 'the Championship' – but West Ham won the Second Division leagues and got promoted in both 1958 and 1981!

2 SECOND DIVISION PLAY-OFFS

Each year, four teams who don't win the Second Division can still go up to the top league if they win the 'Play-Offs' – and West Ham United did just that in 2005 and 2012!

OTHER TROPHIES!

1 x **FA Charity Shield**
1 x **Football League War Cup**
3 x **FA Youth Cup**

Thames Ironworks 1895

1964 FA Cup

1965 Cup Winners' Cup

1975 FA Cup

1980 FA Cup

1999 Intertoto Cup

2012 Play-Offs

125 YEARS
OF WEST HAM UNITED:
RECORD HOLDERS!

These players have all done some amazing things in a Claret and Blue shirt – in fact, their achievements have never been beaten at West Ham!

799

APPEARANCES FOR BILLY BONDS MBE, who played for West Ham for 21 years - between 1967 and 1988. He even has part of the London Stadium named after him!

326

GOALS FOR VIC WATSON, who scored them all for West Ham between 1920 and 1935. He cost just £50 to sign from Wellingborough Town, and he went on to score an amazing 13 hat-tricks as a Hammer!

10-0

WAS THE SCORE WHEN WEST HAM BEAT BURY in the Milk Cup on 25 October 1983! The two teams had played three weeks earlier and West Ham had won 2-1 – but the Hammers hit ten goals this time, with striker Tony Cottee scoring four.

20

MINUTES is all it took for striker Brian Dear to score FIVE goals against West Bromwich Albion in April 1965 – a record in English football. That's one goal every four minutes!

5

HAMMER OF THE YEAR awards were won by Sir Trevor Brooking between 1972 and 1984 – a West Ham record!

59,988

PEOPLE were at London Stadium in March 2019 to watch West Ham play against Everton – a club record!

6

GOALS is the most any West Ham player has scored in a single game – firstly by Vic Watson against Leeds in 1929, and then by Geoff Hurst against Sunderland in 1968!

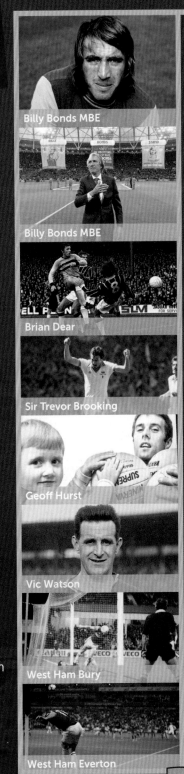

Billy Bonds MBE

Billy Bonds MBE

Brian Dear

Sir Trevor Brooking

Geoff Hurst

Vic Watson

West Ham Bury

West Ham Everton

125 YEARS OF WEST HAM UNITED: MANAGERS!

When West Ham United were first formed, the team was chosen by a committee vote each game! Now, it's the job of the manager – and we've had 17 in our 125-year history.

1902 – 1932:
SYD KING:
Our first-ever manager was also a West Ham player for his first year! King took us to the 1923 FA Cup Final.

1932 – 1950:
CHARLIE PAYNTER

1950 – 1961:
TED FENTON:
Fenton won our first-ever league trophy – the 1957/58 Division Two title.

1961 – 1974:
RON GREENWOOD:
A golden era for West Ham - Greenwood won the 1964 FA Cup and 1965 European Cup Winners' Cup, and reached the 1966 League Cup Final!

1974 – 1989:
JOHN LYALL:
Lyall won the 1975 and 1980 FA Cups, and produced our highest-ever finish in the league (third in 1985/86).

1989 – 1990:
LOU MACARI

1990 – 1994:
BILLY BONDS

1994 – 2001:
HARRY REDKNAPP:
Redknapp won the 1998/99 UEFA Intertoto Cup for West Ham, and achieved our highest-ever Premier League finish (fifth in 1998/1999).

2001 – 2003:
GLENN ROEDER

2003 – 2006:
ALAN PARDEW:
Pardew's West Ham won the Championship Play-Offs in 2005 and reached the 2006 FA Cup Final!

2006 – 2008:
ALAN CURBISHLEY

2008 – 2010:
GIANFRANCO ZOLA:
Our first non-British manager!

2010 – 2011:
AVRAM GRANT

2011 – 2015:
SAM ALLARDYCE:
Allardyce's West Ham won the Championship Play-Offs in 2012.

2015 – 2017:
SLAVEN BILIC

2018 – 2019:
MANUEL PELLEGRINI

2017 – 2018 & 2019 – PRESENT:
DAVID MOYES:
Our current manager is in his second spell as Hammers boss.

Syd King

Charlie Paynter

Ted Fenton

Ron Greenwood

John Lyall

Harry Redknapp

Alan Pardew

Gianfranco Zola

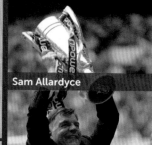
Sam Allardyce

10

125 YEARS
OF WEST HAM UNITED:
KITS & CRESTS!

In 2020/21, the Hammers are playing in a specially designed Commemorative 125th Anniversary Umbro Home kit!

This kit brings back memories of West Ham's greatest achievements in the 1960s, including the creation of our world-famous Academy, our FA Cup and European Cup Winners' Cup wins – and Bobby Moore, Sir Geoff Hurst and Martin Peters leading England to World Cup victory in 1966!

Here are just some of the other famous kits from West Ham's past.

1895: West Ham's first-ever shirts, shorts and socks – when they were still Thames Ironworks FC – were actually all dark blue!

1896: The first-ever 'Thames Ironworks FC' crest!

1903: The first West Ham kit where the main colour was claret. Before then, our kits were mainly blue or white – with a claret stripe or two!

1923: The Club wore a badge for the first time on their kit for the 1923 FA Cup Final – the first time we ever wore the 'crossed Hammers'.

1960s: The classic 1960s kit in which Bobby Moore made his debut and West Ham won the FA Cup and European Cup Winners' Cup.

1970s: A lot of West Ham fans love this iconic kit, which the team wore in their 1975 FA Cup Final victory.

1985: This classic kit was worn for two years, between 1985 and 1987, when West Ham finished third in the top league – their highest-ever position!

1994: West Ham's first-ever kit in the Premier League was a popular one with fans!

2015: The West Ham kit for 2014/15 – our last season at the old stadium, the Boleyn Ground.

2016: West Ham's new badge from 2016, marking the Club's move to the amazing London Stadium.

IRONS

1895 Kit

1896
Thames Ironworks FC Crest

1903 Kit

1923 Kit

1958 Crest

1960s Kit
Bobby Moore debut shirt

1965 Kit

1975 Kit

1985 Kit

1985 Kit

1994 Kit

2015 Kit

WEST HAM UNITED
LONDON

2016

125 YEARS
OF WEST HAM UNITED:
TOP 10 MATCHES!

We've played in some incredible games over our 125-year history – here are just 10 of our greatest-ever matches.

#10
West Ham 3-0 NK Domzale (2016): Our first-ever competitive game at London Stadium was a 3-0 win in the Europa League against NK Domzale from Slovenia - watched live by over 50,000 people!

#9
West Ham 8-1 Newcastle United (1986): Our best-ever season saw us thrash Newcastle and nearly end up winning the league. Our defender, Alvin Martin, scored a hat-trick in this game!

#8
West Ham 2-3 Juventus (2016): It might seem strange to include a game we lost in this list, but this was the day London Stadium opened to West Ham fans with a thrilling opening ceremony and friendly match.

#7
West Ham 3-2 Preston North End (1964): A last-minute goal from Ronnie Boyce helped us win the first major trophy in our history – the 1964 FA Cup!

#6
Blackpool 1-2 West Ham (2012): In the 2012 Championship Play-Off Final, Blackpool were holding us to a draw – until Ricardo Vaz Te scored amazingly in the 87th minute! West Ham were back in the Premier League!

#5
West Ham 2-0 Fulham (1975): Our second-ever FA Cup arrived thanks to two second-half goals from Alan Taylor at Wembley!

#4
West Ham 3-1 Eintracht Frankfurt (1976): The Hammers reached their second European Cup Winners' Cup Final with this amazing comeback win at the Boleyn Ground in 1976.

#3
West Ham 1-0 Arsenal (1980): We were the underdogs against much-fancied Arsenal in the 1980 FA Cup Final – but Sir Trevor Brooking's headed goal in the 13th minute meant the cup was decorated with Claret and Blue!

#2
West Ham 3-2 Manchester United (2016): Our last-ever game at the Boleyn Ground was an awesome one; Winston Reid scored a dramatic, late, winning goal as we beat Manchester United in this five-goal thriller!

#1
West Ham 2-0 1860 Munich (1965): Our biggest-ever trophy and greatest-ever game came at Wembley Stadium in 1965. Alan Sealey scored twice in the second half to win us the European Cup Winners' Cup!

IRONS

125 YEARS
OF WEST HAM UNITED:
10 FASCINATING FACTS!

1 West Ham are one of only eight teams to have always played in the top two divisions in English football.

2 In 1901, after a booking error, West Ham had to play two matches in one day! The Hammers' first team lost 1-0 to Tottenham, but we sent our reserves to Leyton – and won 1-0!

3 We played in the first-ever FA Cup Final at Wembley, in 1923. It was nicknamed the "White Horse Final" because of a police horse called Billie!

4 Only two players have ever scored a penalty with both their left and right foot in the Premier League – and one of them is former Hammer, Bobby Zamora!

5 West Ham scored in 27 consecutive European matches between 1964 and 1980. The only team who have beaten that were Barcelona in 2011!

6 West Ham have been the last team to win the FA Cup while in the second division ever since we beat Arsenal 1-0 in 1980!

7 There have been seven sets of brothers who have played football for West Ham, most recently Rio and Anton Ferdinand.

8 In 1965, Hammers fans were having trouble getting hold of match programmes – so they decided to take their own with them to a match in Greece!

9 Before West Ham moved to London Stadium in 2016, they played at four other grounds: Hermit Road (until 1896), Browning Road (until 1897), Memorial Grounds (until 1904) and Boleyn Ground (until 2016).

10 Three Hammers were in the England squad which won the 1966 World Cup: Martin Peters, Bobby Moore, and Geoff Hurst – who scored a hat-trick in the Final!

2019/20
SEASON REVIEW
IN GOALS!

The longest-ever season in West Ham United and Premier League history, 2019/20 saw some amazing wins, amazing drama – and, of course, amazing GOALS!

PRE-SEASON

Looking to build on a tenth-place finish, West Ham United bolstered their squad by spending big under then-manager Manuel Pellegrini during pre-season.

This included the record signing of tall French striker Sebastien Haller from Eintracht Frankfurt and the acquisition of skilful midfielder Pablo Fornals from Villarreal!

AUGUST 2019

GOAL OF THE MONTH:
Sebastien Haller vs Watford

Haller and the Hammers recovered from a first-day loss to champions Manchester City and a 1-1 draw at Brighton to soar past Watford at Vicarage Road!

This brilliant overhead kick from our record signing put the gloss on a brilliant 3-1 away win.

The Frenchman went on to score his first goal at London Stadium against Norwich in his next game, the Irons cruising past the Canaries 2-0!

RESULTS & SCORERS

10 August: 0-5 L **v Manchester City (H)** — PL

17 August: 1-1 D **v Brighton & Hove Albion (A)** — PL — Chicharito 61

24 August: 3-1 W **v Watford (A)** — PL — Noble 3 (pen), Haller 64, 73

27 August: 2-0 W **v Newport County (A)** — LC — Wilshere 43, Fornals 65

31 August: 2-0 W **v Norwich City (H)** — PL — Haller 24, Yarmolenko 56

SEPTEMBER 2019

GOAL OF THE MONTH:
Aaron Cresswell vs Manchester United

The Irons kicked off September unable to break down a stubborn Aston Villa side in a tough 0-0 draw away from home.

But London Stadium was soon roaring once again – a well-taken Andriy Yarmolenko strike, and this beautiful 25-yard free-kick from Aaron Cresswell, sealed a 2-0 win over Manchester United and sent us up to fifth in the table!

To cap things off, Yarmo and Cress were both on the mark again for a second week in a row, both finding the back of the net as we played out an entertaining 2-2 draw at Bournemouth.

RESULTS & SCORERS

16 September: 0-0 D **v Aston Villa (A)** - PL

22 September: 2-0 W **v Manchester United (H)** — PL — Yarmolenko 44, Cresswell 84

25 September: 0-4 L **v Oxford United (A)** — LC

28 September: 2-2 D **v Bournemouth (A)** — PL — Yarmolenko 10, Cresswell 74

OCTOBER 2019

GOAL OF THE MONTH:
Sebastien Haller vs Crystal Palace

The Hammers endured a difficult month in October, but they still put together a fantastic team goal to take the lead against Crystal Palace at London Stadium.

Eight of West Ham's ten outfield players were involved in the 12 passes which released Ryan Fredericks down the wing, and when the right-back played the ball low into the penalty area, there was Haller to steer it in.

Sadly, Palace completed a second-half comeback to win 2-1 and end the Hammers' good run of form, which was compounded by a 2-0 loss at Everton two weeks later.

The Irons finished the month with a battling 1-1 draw against Sheffield United, who equalised late on after Robert Snodgrass had put the home team ahead in the first half.

RESULTS & SCORERS

5 October: 1-2 L **v Crystal Palace (H)** — PL — Haller 54
19 October: 0-2 L **v Everton (A)** — PL
26 October: 1-1 D **v Sheffield United (H)** — PL — Snodgrass 44

NOVEMBER 2019

GOAL OF THE MONTH:
Aaron Cresswell vs Chelsea

Results didn't always seem to match the fight that the Irons showed in November, but Cresswell's great goal ended the month on a high.

After going three goals behind to Newcastle United and Tottenham Hotspur, West Ham almost managed to complete two late comebacks, but fell just short on both occasions.

As a result, the Irons went to Chelsea's stadium, Stamford Bridge, as underdogs, having not won there since 2003.

But they left with a win, thanks to some incredible defending, an unforgettable debut from goalkeeper David Martin — and Cresswell's crucial winning goal. The No3 collected a pass from Fornals, cut inside onto his right foot and fired the ball into the bottom corner.

RESULTS & SCORERS

2 November: 2-3 L v Newcastle United (H) — PL — Balbuena 73, Snodgrass 90

9 November: 0-3 L v Burnley (A) — PL

23 November: 2-3 L v Tottenham Hotspur (H) — PL — Antonio 73, Ogbonna 90+6

30 November: 1-0 W v Chelsea (A) — PL — Cresswell 48

COME ON YOU IRONS

DECEMBER 2019

GOAL OF THE MONTH:
Sebastien Haller vs Southampton

Frustrations continued for the Hammers in December, with four narrow defeats from their five league games, but Haller's winner at Southampton at least brought about some festive cheer in time for Christmas!

The Frenchman took one look at Fornals' headed knock-down and slammed the ball into the ground, his shot skipping up and finding the far corner — the goalkeeper had no chance!

RESULTS & SCORERS

4 December: 0-2 L v Wolverhampton Wanderers (A) — PL

9 December: 1-3 L v Arsenal (H) — PL — Ogbonna 38

14 December: 1-0 W v Southampton (A) — PL — Haller 37

26 December: 1-2 L v Crystal Palace (A) — PL — Snodgrass 57

28 December: 1-2 L v Leicester (H) — PL — Fornals 45

The turn of the year saw a change in management as West Ham United parted ways with Manuel Pellegrini. On 29 December 2019, the Club reappointed former manager David Moyes, who had guided the Irons to a 13th-place finish two years earlier.

JANUARY 2020

GOAL OF THE MONTH:
Mark Noble vs Bournemouth

Moyes got off to the perfect start in his second spell in charge, with West Ham thrashing Bournemouth 4-0 on New Year's Day 2020!

Captain Mark Noble scored the all-important first goal with this deflected shot, and it was added to by a penalty from the skipper, another Haller bicycle kick and a Felipe Anderson solo goal.

In the FA Cup, West Ham saw off League One challengers Gillingham through goals from the two Pablos – Zabaleta and Fornals – before being eliminated by West Bromwich Albion.

The rest of the month saw the Irons held to a 1-1 draw by Moyes' former side, Everton, while West Ham could consider themselves unlucky in hard-fought Premier League losses to Sheffield United and Liverpool.

RESULTS & SCORERS

1 January: 4-0 W v Bournemouth (H) – PL – Noble 17, 35 (pen.), Haller 25, Anderson 66
5 January: 2-0 W v Gillingham (A) – FA – Zabaleta 74, Fornals 90+4
10 January: 0-1 L v Sheffield United (A) – PL
18 January: 1-1 D v Everton (H) – PL – Diop 40
22 January: 1-4 L v Leicester (A) – PL – Noble 50 (pen.)
25 January: 0-1 L v West Bromwich Albion (H) – FA
29 January: 0-2 L v Liverpool (H) – PL

FEBRUARY 2020

GOAL OF THE MONTH:
Jarrod Bowen vs Southampton

West Ham's fightback began in earnest in February.

The team were bolstered by two late arrivals in the transfer window: midfielder Tomas Soucek from Slavia Prague and forward Jarrod Bowen from Hull City.

Soucek's debut came in a 3-3 thriller against Brighton & Hove Albion, in which Snodgrass scored two emphatic volleys to put the Irons in a commanding position, only for Brighton to hit back late on and claim a point.

After losing to then-champions Manchester City, Moyes' men came within 22 minutes of being the first team to beat eventual Premier League winners Liverpool, only for the Reds to score twice late on at Anfield and turn things around.

Then came a special day for Bowen, as our new No17 chipped the Southampton goalkeeper after just 15 minutes on his London Stadium debut. Further goals from Haller and Antonio had the Claret and Blue army leaping to their feet in delight – the Hammers were back on song.

RESULTS & SCORERS

1 February: 3-3 D v **Brighton & Hove Albion (H)** – PL – **Diop 30, Snodgrass 45, 57**
19 February: 0-2 L v **Manchester City (A)** – PL
24 February: 2-3 L v **Liverpool (A)** – PL – **Diop 12, Fornals 54**
29 February: 3-1 W v **Southampton (H)** – PL – **Bowen 15, Haller 40, Antonio 54**

WEST HAM UNITED FOOTBALL CO LTD

MARCH 2020

Nothing could have prepared any Hammer for the way the world changed in March.

The Hammers' first – and only – game of the month saw them create plenty of chances at Arsenal, only to come up against the Gunners' keeper Bernd Leno in inspired form, before Arsenal won it late on.

It was our last football match for 105 days.

The impact of the COVID-19 global pandemic meant that all Premier League football was delayed for three months to keep everyone as safe as possible.

As football took an enforced break, the entire West Ham family – Moyes, his players, the staff and all our supporters – were instead united in supporting the NHS staff and other key workers who kept the country running during a very difficult time.

Each and every one of them remains a true West Ham United hero.

RESULTS & SCORERS

7 March: 0-1 L v **Arsenal (A)** - PL

HAMMERS FINISH OFF WITH GOALS GALORE!

In June 2020, Premier League matches – after an unprecedented pause – restarted across the country.

Football was back, and although the pandemic meant that supporters weren't allowed inside stadia to see the games, there were still plenty of ways Hammers fans could cheer on their side from home.

And cheer they did, as Moyes' men hit the goal trail in June and July, scoring 14 times in their last nine matches to end the season on a real high!

JUNE 2020

West Ham's first match back was against Wolverhampton Wanderers at London Stadium, some 97 days after the game was originally due to be played.

It was only the second time West Ham had ever played a competitive game without any fans in their history, but a tight and tense match swung Wolves' way late on.

A similar story arose at Tottenham Hotspur just three days later – but Moyes' Hammers were on the cusp of hitting a special run of form...

JULY 2020

GOALS OF THE MONTH:
Andriy Yarmolenko vs Chelsea
Michail Antonio vs Norwich City
Declan Rice vs Watford

The Irons scored so many goals in July, we could hardly choose just one!

The month began as it would go on – with thrills, goals and lots of drama!

After falling behind to Chelsea at London Stadium following a controversial Video Assistant Referee (VAR) decision, West Ham came back fighting – and substitute Andriy Yarmolenko capped a stunning 3-2 comeback with this last-minute winner!

Then, after being unlucky to come away with just a point from matches against Newcastle and Burnley – both of which the Hammers dominated, in truth – Antonio enjoyed the game of his life.

The striker bagged all four goals – a volley (pictured), two headers and a close-range finish – against Norwich in a virtuoso display at Carrow Road.

But 'the Beast' wasn't done there, as Antonio went on to score the opening goals against both Watford (in a 3-1 win) and Manchester United (in a 1-1 draw) which mathematically confirmed the Hammers' Premier League place for the season ahead.

That win over Watford also saw captain Mark Noble make his 500th appearance for his boyhood Club, a landmark celebrated in style by his midfield partner Declan Rice, whose 25-yard thunderbolt of a shot sealed the win.

Finishing off with a draw against Aston Villa, the Hammers ultimately lost just one of their last seven games in the Premier League after an incredibly strong run of performances and results from Moyes' men.

After a one-of-a-kind season, everybody wearing Claret and Blue could look forward to blowing bubbles in 2020/21 with excitement and optimism – the West Ham way.

RESULTS & SCORERS

20 June: 0-2 L v **Wolverhampton Wanderers (H)** – PL

23 June: 0-2 L v **Tottenham Hotspur (A)** – PL

1 July: 3-2 W v **Chelsea (H)** – PL – Soucek 45+2, Antonio 51, Yarmolenko 89

5 July: 2-2 D v **Newcastle United (A)** – PL – Antonio 4, Soucek 65

8 July: 0-1 L v **Burnley (H)** – PL

11 July: 4-0 W v **Norwich (A)** – PL – Antonio 11, 45+1, 54, 74

17 July: 3-1 W v **Watford (H)** – PL – Antonio 6, Soucek 10, Rice 36

22 July: 1-1 D v **Manchester United (A)** – PL – Antonio 45+2 (pen.)

26 July: 1-1 D v **Aston Villa (H)** – PL – Yarmolenko 85

ANTONIO'S AWESOME JULY!

BY THE NUMBERS

7 Appearances

8 Goals

1 Assist

4 Goals against Norwich – the first Hammer ever to score four in a Premier League game!

1 Premier League Player of the Month award

"Michail has been really, really important to us. He's played great and he has matured a lot recently. He's looking after himself in a way that gives him every chance of performing well and he's certainly stepped up to the plate. I'm really pleased for him."

DAVID MOYES

PREDICTION TIME!

What do you think will happen in the world of football in 2021?

Write down you and your best friend's predictions – and then come back at the end of the season and see how many you both got right!

1 Where West Ham United will finish in the 2020/21 Premier League:

I THINK: No.5

MY FRIEND THINKS:

2 West Ham United's top scorer in 2020/21 will be:

I THINK: Bowen

MY FRIEND THINKS:

3 Our Hammer of the Year (best player) in 2020/21 will be:

I THINK: rice or bowen

MY FRIEND THINKS:

4 The 2020/21 Premier League champions will be:

I THINK: Man city

MY FRIEND THINKS:

22\23

5 The 2020/21 Premier League top scorer will be:

I THINK: Haaland

MY FRIEND THINKS:

6 The 2021 FA Cup winners will be:

I THINK: Liverpool

MY FRIEND THINKS:

7 The 2021 EFL Cup winners will be:

I THINK: ?

MY FRIEND THINKS:

8 The 2021 UEFA Champions League winners will be:

I THINK: Real madrid

MY FRIEND THINKS:

9 The 2021 Europa League winners will be:

I THINK: Francfurt

MY FRIEND THINKS:

10 The European Championship winners will be:

I THINK: Fuham

MY FRIEND THINKS:

MY SCORE: 9 /10   MY FRIEND'S SCORE: 0 /10

DREAM TEAM

Every fan out there wants to manage West Ham United — and now, we're letting you do just that!

If you could buy any players in the world, who would you want to see in Claret and Blue? Michail up front with Messi? How about Jarrod Bowen on the right wing, with Cristiano Ronaldo on the left?

Pick your dream West Ham team below!

GOALKEEPER

GOALKEEPER
Areola

DEFENDERS

RIGHT-BACK	CENTRE-BACK	CENTRE-BACK	LEFT-BACK
Emerson Palmieri	Kurt Zouma	Thilo Kehrer	Nayef Aguerd

MIDFIELDERS

RIGHT WING	CENTRE MIDFIELD	CENTRE MIDFIELD	LEFT WING
Saïd Benrahma	Tomáš Souček	Declan Rice	Maxwell Cornet

FORWARDS

STRIKER	STRIKER
Antonio	Scamacca

WHO'S BEHIND

Somebody's been messing around with the filters on Instagram again!

Take a look at these photos of players and moments from 2019/20. Can you name the players in each of them?

Some of them are pretty tricky – but you can do it!

1
Who's this Hammer at the training ground?

Antonio

2
This player's left foot could paint a beautiful watercolour for sure!

Cresswell

3
Much like a ninja, this defender's quiet – but effective!

issa diop

4
This Iron makes no shortage of blocks at the back!

randolph

THE FILTERS?

5
This man's well known for his deliveries – but usually from set pieces!

ANSWER

6
A real-life superhero for the West Ham women's team!

ANSWER

7
This snap's been turned negative – but the moment itself couldn't have been more positive!

ANSWER

8
A portrait of West Ham's future in terms of this young Academy graduate!

ANSWER Ben Jonson

9
Always joining up the dots at the back for West Ham women, it's...

Coventry

10
Even Mona Lisa couldn't stop this Hammer from smiling!

ANSWER

IRONS INSIDER: LUKASZ FABIANSKI!

Get the inside scoop on some of your favourite Irons – like Polish international goalkeeper, Lukasz Fabianski!

FULL NAME:
Lukasz Marek Fabianski

BORN:
18 April 1985

PLACE OF BIRTH:
Kostrzyn nad Odrą, Poland

NICKNAME:
'Super Fab'

With 13 distinguished years in English football behind him, Lukasz Fabianski has developed into one of the most revered, respected and reliable 'keepers around in the Premier League.

Having been named Hammer of the Year at the end of his first season with the Irons in 2018/19, the Polish shot-stopper is a popular figure amongst the Claret and Blue Army with his sharp reflexes and commanding presence in his area.

WHAT THEY SAY ABOUT HIM:

"What impresses me about him is that he exudes calmness. Lukasz never seems to get flustered and that's important. As a goalkeeper, you need to have a calm head on your shoulders. If you start losing that control, that can quickly spread to the defenders in front of you."

PHIL PARKES, former West Ham goalkeeper

INSIDER FACT:

Officially, Lukasz speaks two languages – Polish and English – but he's been trying to learn words and phrases from his Spanish team-mates as well, like Pablo Fornals!

CAREER HISTORY:

Lech Poznan (2004-2005)
Legia Warsaw (2005-2007)
Arsenal (2007-2014)
Swansea City (2014-2018)
West Ham United (2018-present)

STAT ATTACK!
2019/20:

25 Premier League appearances
2,119 minutes played
72 saves
100 throw outs
192 goal kicks
1 penalty saved

PREMIER LEAGUE CAREER:

244 appearances
63 clean sheets
806 saves
2,004 goal kicks taken

*Stats correct as of end of 2019/20 Premier League season

IRONS INSIDER: DARREN RANDOLPH!

Darren Randolph rejoined the Club from Middlesbrough in January 2020 – but how much do you know about the Republic of Ireland goalie?

FULL NAME:
Darren Edward Andrew Randolph

BORN:
12 May 1987

PLACE OF BIRTH:
Bray, Ireland

NICKNAME:
'Randz'

Now in his second spell with West Ham United, Darren Randolph returns to east London with some incredible recollections of guarding the Irons' net – not least his brilliant performance in the historic final game at Boleyn Ground in May 2016, a 3-2 win over Manchester United.

Renowned for his lightning-fast reflexes and excellent distribution, Randolph played 42 times for West Ham between 2015 and 2017 before moving on to Middlesbrough.

Becoming a Hammer once more in January 2020, Randolph is ready to fight for the chance to make more memories between the sticks as David Moyes' starting 'keeper.

WHAT HE SAYS:

"It feels great to be back. This is a massive Club, the potential it has. The fans are fantastic and there's obviously a great changing room as well. When things are going well here, it's just brilliant to be a part of."

INSIDER FACT:

Darren not only played in the last-ever game at Boleyn Ground in May 2016, he also started the first-ever match at London Stadium – a 3-0 Europa League qualifying win over Slovenian side NK Domzale – in August of that year. He was also in goal for our 3-0 win over current champions Liverpool in 2015 – our first win at Anfield in 52 years!

STAT ATTACK!
2019/20:

2 Premier League appearances

14 Championship appearances (for Middlesbrough)

1440 minutes played (combined)

16 accurate long balls

PREMIER LEAGUE CAREER:

31 appearances
6 clean sheets
85 saves
839 passes
262 goal kicks

*Stats correct as of end of 2019/20 Premier League season

CAREER HISTORY:

Charlton Athletic (2004-2010, including loans)
Motherwell (2010-2013)
Birmingham City (2013-2015)
West Ham United (2015-2017, 2020-present)
Middlesbrough (2017-2020)

IRONS INSIDER:
ANGELO OGBONNA!

Often seen battling away at the heart of the Hammers' backline, it's our popular, powerful centre-back, Angelo Ogbonna!

FULL NAME:
Obinze Angelo Ogbonna

BORN:
23 May 1988

PLACE OF BIRTH:
Cassino, Italy

NICKNAME:
'Oggy'

A winner in every sense of the word, Angelo Ogbonna first joined West Ham United from Italian champions Juventus in the summer of 2015.

After starting his career in Italy with Torino and starring for his country on the way to the final of Euro 2012, Ogbonna's time at Juventus saw him win back-to-back Serie A league titles in 2013/14 and 2014/15, as well as the 2014/15 Coppa Italia.

Ever-present, experienced and reliable, 'Oggy' can always be relied upon to make a crucial tackle or headed clearance – or five! – for West Ham, and he fittingly captained the team on several occasions last season.

A model professional and a true Hammer, he'll be looking to bring more personal glory to east London in the years ahead.

WHAT THEY SAY ABOUT HIM:

"I think I've performed consistently well over the last three seasons but for me, this year, I think Hammer of the Year would have been Ogbonna! He's been a rock, solid, he has taken his game to another level and is getting better with age and he's a leader around the team. The lads love him so, for me, it would have gone to him."

DECLAN RICE

INSIDER FACT:
An adopted east Londoner, when tested on his Cockney rhyming slang, Oggy was on the mark with "bees and honey" (money), "skin and blister" (sister) and "dog and bone" (phone) – but couldn't quite understand "I kicked it in the sausage roll" (goal) or "use your loaf" (head)!

STAT ATTACK!
2019/20:
31 Premier League appearances
130 clearances
65 headed clearances
102 aerial battles won
2 goals

PREMIER LEAGUE CAREER:

135 appearances
677 clearances
576 recoveries
618 duels won

*Stats correct as of end of 2019/20 Premier League season

CAREER HISTORY:

Torino (2006-2013, including loan)
Juventus (2013-2015)
West Ham United (2015-present)

IRONS INSIDER: BEN JOHNSON!

An Academy of Football graduate set to make a massive impact in 2020/21, Ben Johnson represents the future of our defence in Claret and Blue!

FULL NAME:
Benjamin Anthony Johnson

BORN:
24 January 2000

PLACE OF BIRTH:
Waltham Forest, England

NICKNAME:
'Jonno'

Ben Johnson's West Ham United debut was the stuff of footballing dreams: at 19 years old, he was chosen to start against the stars of Manchester City in February 2019.

Although Johnson and the Hammers didn't quite manage to hold Sergio Aguero and the eventual champions at bay that day, his impressive performance had everybody talking: here was a young defender with bags of obvious talent.

The nephew of former England full-back Paul Parker – and cousin of former England defender Ledley King – Johnson is comfortable playing on either side of defence.

He picked up where he left off towards the end of 2019/20 with some rock-solid displays at full-back, and is certain to get plenty more opportunities this season – so don't be surprised to see him take them once again!

WHAT THEY SAY ABOUT HIM:

"Ben is a tremendous athlete and is mentally very good. We are really proud of him at the Academy because he is everything we would talk about. He is the right type of character, he stays late in the afternoons to get better and is diligent in his work. He is hungry for more success and everyone at the Academy is proud and delighted for him."
TERRY WESTLEY, former Academy Manager

INSIDER FACT:

Johnson has been with West Ham since he was just seven-years-old! A popular character around the dressing room, he likes to spend his free time watching TV and films and listening to 80s soul and gospel music – he's a massive fan of Kirk Franklin!

STAT ATTACK!
2019/20:

3 Premier League appearances
10 clearances
17 duels won
3 interceptions

PREMIER LEAGUE CAREER:

4 appearances
9 tackles
4 interceptions
13 clearances
13 recoveries

*Stats correct as of end of 2019/20 Premier League season

WEST HAM
TEASERS!
CLARET OR BLUE?

We've got some 50-50 questions here to test your knowledge of all things West Ham United. All you have to do is guess which answer is correct: the Claret one, or the Blue?

Who was West Ham United's top goalscorer in the 2019/20 season?

| MICHAIL ANTONIO | SEBASTIEN HALLER |

Who won the Hammer of the Year award in 2020?

| MARK NOBLE | DECLAN RICE |

Who is the Club's all-time top goalscorer?

| SIR GEOFF HURST | VIC WATSON |

What is the name of the West Ham United mascot?

| HAMMERMAN | HAMMERHEAD |

How many permanent managers have West Ham United had in their history?

| 16 | 17 |

What is the name of the band who sing 'I'm Forever Blowing Bubbles'?

| THE COCKNEY LADS | THE COCKNEY REJECTS |

In which year did West Ham first win the FA Cup?

| 1964 | 1975 |

Which left-footed player made more appearances for West Ham in 2019/20?

| AARON CRESSWELL | ROBERT SNODGRASS |

ANAGRAMS

Can you unscramble the letters to form some West Ham-related players past and present? (Clue: Ignore the position of the spaces – the words in the answers may be shorter or longer than in the anagrams!)

CLEAN DICER

BARK MELON

ROMEO

OASIS DIP

AID COIN

OAK COSTUMES

THE FOGS FUR

THE WEST HAM
WORDSEARCH

These **20** West Ham-related words are all hidden somewhere in the grid below! *How many of them can you find?*

```
Q Y R A S R E V I N N A M Z A
Y M O A K D P E U L B U U E X
S U M O Y E S Y M E D A C A O
D I E G V Z K B U B B L E S V
Q D W G A O I N O T N A M D N
K A N O D N O L T S A E F T X
L T P R E M I E R L E A G U E
I S L A G P W S O 2020 C E K N
N N Z P E L B O N L E A C V N
J O I R O N S T Q N Y V E Q H
Q D H U R S T N O S N H O J K
Q N D E T I N U M A H T S E W
G O O M H D B O W E N Z C Z Z
M L M A T C H W L K Q W D E M
A O B O N D S I C L A R E T E
```

☐ ACADEMY	☐ CLARET	☐ MATCH
☐ ANNIVERSARY	☐ EAST LONDON	☐ MOYES
☐ ANTONIO	☐ GOAL	☐ NOBLE
☐ BLUE	☐ HURST	☐ PREMIER LEAGUE
☐ BONDS	☐ IRONS	☐ SOUCEK
☐ BOWEN	☐ JOHNSON	☐ WEST HAM UNITED
☐ BUBBLES	☐ LONDON STADIUM	

125 YEARS TOGETHER

1895   2020

UNITED FOREVER

WEST HAM UNITED FOOTBALL CLUB

COMMEMORATIVE 125TH ANNIVERSARY

AWAY KIT 2020/21

umbro

MR WEST HAM:
MARK NOBLE'S
500 APPEARANCES

On Friday 17 July, captain Mark Noble led West Ham United out of the tunnel for his 500th appearance for his boyhood club. Here, we look back and celebrate a modern-day Claret and Blue legend!

FACT FILE:

CAREER HISTORY:

West Ham United (2004-present; 502 appearances, 60 goals)

LOANS:

Hull City (2006; 5 appearances)
Ipswich Town (2006; 13 appearances, 1 goal)

*Stats correct as of end of 2019/20 Premier League season

BIOGRAPHY:

Born in nearby Canning Town, east London, 'Nobes' first joined the Academy of Football in 2000, going on to become the youngest player to appear for the West Ham reserve team in 2003 at just 15-years old.

In 2004, he made his senior West Ham debut and, following two loan spells in 2006, established himself as a Claret and Blue regular in 2007/08 under Alan Curbishley.

Ever since then, he has been a consistent performer in the Irons' midfield for over 15 years, with goals galore, two Hammer of the Year awards, two promotions to the Premier League and an iconic status around the Club.

Alongside his skill, he has grown up to epitomise everything that the Irons are all about with his will to work, his never-say-die attitude and his sheer love of playing for West Ham United.

FULL NAME:
Mark James Noble
BORN:
8 May 1987
PLACE OF BIRTH:
Canning Town, London, England
NICKNAME:
'Nobes'

> 17 or 18 years ago I was standing outside Upton Park, trying to sneak in and asking for players' shirts and here I am playing 500 games, Club captain and I've been part of this Club for many years. I'll never forget it.
>
> MARK NOBLE

NOBES BY NUMBERS

The **10th** player to play 500 first-team games for West Ham United

460 starts; **40** substitute appearances

60 goals – **38** of which were penalties

380 Premier League appearances – a West Ham record

217 times Noble shared the pitch with Carlton Cole – his most regular teammate

6-0 was Nobes' biggest win – against Brighton & Hove Albion on 14 April 2012 at Boleyn Ground

INSIDER FACT:

As of 2020, Noble had the second-highest conversion rate amongst regular penalty takers in the world in the last 20 years. His success rate of 90.5% was only beaten by Bayern Munich striker Robert Lewandowski (91.1%).

6 OF MARK'S MILESTONE MATCHES!

The man you want for the big occasion, Mark Noble can always be relied upon to step up when it matters, as he has done so often in his first 500 games for the Club.

HERE ARE JUST SIX EXAMPLES...

MATCH #1:
vs Southend United, Tuesday 24 August 2004
Noble made his West Ham debut as a 17-year-old in the League Cup second round. Fresh-faced but fearless, the future captain impressed many. He could not yet drive, though, so he had to run home after the Hammers' 2-0 win!

MATCH #29:
vs Tottenham Hotspur, Sunday 4 March 2007
Having scored his first goal in Claret and Blue in the FA Cup against Brighton in his previous game, Noble's first Premier League goal was one to remember – a sweetly-struck volley against London rivals Tottenham!

MATCH #38:
vs Manchester United, Sunday 13 May 2007
West Ham needed to win at Manchester United on the last day of the season to have any chance of staying up in the Premier League. Nobes fought tooth and nail for every loose ball in midfield, playing a massive part in the Hammers' 1-0 win that sealed the 'Great Escape'!

MATCH #219:
vs Blackpool, Saturday 19 May 2012
After being crowned Hammer of the Year, Nobes drove the Hammers to promotion via this thrilling Championship Play-Off Final in 2012 – then drove straight to the airport afterwards to celebrate his upcoming wedding!

MATCH #366:
vs Manchester United, Tuesday 10 May 2016
There was no way West Ham weren't winning the last-ever game at Boleyn Ground with Mark Noble as captain! The skipper was immense – and visibly emotional after the final whistle – as the Irons came from behind to famously win 3-2.

MATCH #500:
vs Watford, Friday 17 July 2020
The skipper played a massive part in last season's crucial 3-1 win over Watford at London Stadium – but what else would you expect from him on a landmark occasion?

MARK NOBLE – IN THEIR WORDS...

The captain's numbers speak for themselves — but what do the people who know Mark Noble best have to say about him?

"On behalf of everyone at West Ham United, we would like to congratulate and salute Mark Noble on the magnificent achievement of his 500th senior appearance for the Club.

"Mark becomes only the tenth player in our 125-year history to reach the milestone and a look at the nine figures alongside him proves just how momentous a feat it is.

"Vic Watson, Jimmy Ruffell, Bobby Moore, Geoff Hurst, Billy Bonds, Frank Lampard Sr, Trevor Brooking, Alvin Martin and Steve Potts: all fantastic servants to West Ham United and names that will forever be remembered as legends in the Claret and Blue.

"Mark Noble quite rightly takes his place among those legends."

DAVID SULLIVAN & DAVID GOLD,
JOINT-CHAIRMEN OF WEST HAM UNITED

"Nowadays to get 500 games for any club is a remarkable achievement. He's been a one-club man and served the club incredibly well since he's been a young player to where he is now. He's still leading the group, still very vocal and still playing well for the team too. Long may it continue."

DAVID MOYES, WEST HAM UNITED MANAGER

"I think what separates him from the rest is that he knows what the Club means over the last 20 years.

"Obviously growing up supporting it as a boy, then coming through the Academy, then playing in the first team, and then going on to lead the team, he knows the full ins and outs; he knows everything about it, he knows the people, and he obviously lives and breathes the Club."

ROBERT SNODGRASS,
WEST HAM UNITED TEAMMATE

"Probably the biggest compliment I can pay him on the pitch is that I think he's a fantastic player, sets the standards every day in training, and that's why he's had such an amazing career: because that will to win, that desire, that enthusiasm and love for the game and the Club is something that's shone out of him from a young age, and that's why he's still playing now."

JACK COLLISON, WHO PLAYED WITH NOBLE AT THE ACADEMY OF FOOTBALL AND 82 TIMES TOGETHER FOR THE FIRST TEAM

"Yes Nobes, yes skipper! I swear down, I can't believe he's reached 500 appearances. I wish him all the best going on, and I hope he gets another 500 more — although that's probably unlikely, unless he's rolling out there with his Zimmer frame!

"I know he's Mr West Ham, but he's more than that. For any players who come into the changing room, he's the one that leads them, guides them — the big father figure that they all need. I've seen it first-hand. Captain. Leader. A great guy and a great person, a great human being, and that's what counts more."

CARLTON COLE, FORMER WEST HAM TEAMMATE
WHO WAS NOBLE'S MOST COMMON TEAMMATE
(217 MUTUAL APPEARANCES)

IRONS INSIDER: TOMAS SOUCEK!

West Ham United's very own midfield man-mountain, Tomas Soucek completed his permanent transfer to the Irons in July 2020 after an impressive six-month loan spell.

FULL NAME:
Tomas Soucek

BORN:
27 February 1995

PLACE OF BIRTH:
Havlíčkův Brod, Czech Republic

NICKNAME:
'Suk'

t first glance, you might think that Tomas Soucek's height and imposing frame are his greatest weapons – but those features belie an adept and athletically gifted footballer.

A recent Czech Footballer of the Year, Soucek is a box-to-box midfielder who, since moving to east London in January 2020, has proven himself more than capable of making a difference at both ends of the pitch in the Premier League.

Soucek rose to the attention of the Hammers' scouting team with his brilliant performances at Sparta Prague – where he won two league titles, two cups and played in the Champions League – and for the Czech Republic, notably starring against England in 2019.

Gelling immediately into the West Ham midfield, Soucek scored three times following the 2019/20 season restart, using both his height with a headed goal against Watford and also his supreme technique to volley home against Newcastle. At €21 million, his transfer represents an outstanding coup for West Ham United.

WHAT THEY SAY ABOUT HIM:

"The biggest concern with Tomas was how well he would start. All the other things connected to him have been good – he can score, run, help us – he's a good footballer. The best thing about him is he is a terrific lad. He has scored some really important goals for us; he could have got a couple more as well. I have to say Tomas has been a really good fit." DAVID MOYES

INSIDER FACT:

Soucek's parents had a massive influence on his career as a footballer – his dad is a huge football fan, and his mum is a marathon runner! That perhaps explains why the Czech Golden Ball winner ran more than 13.1km in only his second Premier League game – more than any other West Ham player in six years!

STAT ATTACK!

2019/20:

13 Premier League appearances
3 goals
394 passes
29 tackles won
Averaging **5.5** headers won per game
Averaging **2.2** tackles and
2.5 interceptions per game

*Stats correct as of end of 2019/20 Premier League season

CAREER HISTORY:

Slavia Prague (2014-2020, including loans)
West Ham United (2020-present)

IRONS INSIDER: PABLO FORNALS!

Combining tireless running with effortless skill, Spanish midfielder Pablo Fornals has established himself as a fans' favourite after just one season in east London!

FULL NAME:
Pablo Fornals Malla

BORN:
22 February 1996

PLACE OF BIRTH:
Castelló de la Plana, Spain

NICKNAME:
'Pablito'

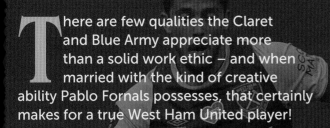

There are few qualities the Claret and Blue Army appreciate more than a solid work ethic — and when married with the kind of creative ability Pablo Fornals possesses, that certainly makes for a true West Ham United player!

Fornals became a Hammer in June 2019 after impressing for his country at the 2019 European Under-21 Championships. He scored two goals en route to the Final, which Fornals started as Spain beat Germany, 2-1.

Weeks later, and Fornals was swapping the technical battles of La Liga with Villarreal for the fast-paced, more physical matches West Ham would face in the Premier League.

While he admits he took a bit of time to adapt to his new surroundings, 'Pablito' put in some seriously impressive showings in Claret and Blue in his debut season — scoring at Anfield, grabbing two assists against Southampton and playing in a variety of positions in the forward line.

Always determined to give his best, there's more where that came from for Pablo Fornals!

WHAT THEY SAY ABOUT HIM:

"The biggest thing I can say about Pablo Fornals is that his work-rate is really honest. I've really liked the boy since I've come here. Pablo has smiled and done the work and I think getting some goals was good for him as well. The big thing is that his running stats are very good for us." DAVID MOYES

INSIDER FACT:

Fornals has adapted seamlessly to being a Londoner! On his days off, he loves to go to city markets at Brick Lane and Shoreditch, open spaces like Hyde Park or Camden, and even the classic landmarks like Tower Bridge. His dog, Kira, who is a cocker spaniel, often goes too!

STAT ATTACK!
2019/20:

36 Premier League appearances
2 goals
5 assists
843 passes
61 crosses
155 recoveries

*Stats correct as of end of 2019/20 Premier League season

CAREER HISTORY:
Malaga (2014-2017)
Villarreal (2017-2019)
West Ham United (2019-present)

37

SPOT THE

Two seemingly identical pictures of David Moyes' Hammers defending a corner kick at the end of last season... but there are **10 differences** between them!

1	NHS
2	
3	
4	
5	

DIFFERENCE! ⚓

How many differences can you find? Write them down on the page as you spot them!

6	
7	
8	
9	
10	

ANSWERS ON PAGES 60-61

IRONS INSIDER: JARROD BOWEN!

Jarrod Bowen has adapted rapidly to life in east London since joining West Ham United from Hull City late on in the January 2020 transfer window, offering plenty of goal threat from out wide!

FULL NAME:
Jarrod Bowen
BORN:
20 December 1996
PLACE OF BIRTH:
Leominster, England

Tricky but terrifically hard-working, winger Bowen is a Hammer whom defenders have found hard to contain!

The young forward is able to mix things up at short notice, offering plenty of menace with his clever running, tireless work ethic, rapid pace — and deadly left foot.

Often playing wide on the right, the sight of Bowen cutting inside to shoot or cross — both often with pinpoint accuracy — has had many Premier League opponents scrambling back in panic!

The No17's chance at impressing in the Premier League was well earned after he racked up 54 goals and 14 assists in his final three seasons at Hull City, after originally being scouted from non-league Hereford.

In his first half-season in Claret and Blue, Bowen not only netted on his home debut against Southampton in February, but also recorded four vital assists as he played an influential role in the Hammers' strong finish to 2019/20.

WHAT THEY SAY ABOUT HIM:

"For me, he's probably my favourite West Ham signing for as long as I can remember. To score the amount of goals he did from a wide area for Hull, it was obvious to me that he could do it in the Premier League. He's got great ability, he makes clever runs and he can finish, but also he's a grafter. That's exactly what West Ham is all about and every player should have those attributes." DEAN ASHTON, FORMER WEST HAM STRIKER

INSIDER FACT:
If things had turned out differently, Jarrod wouldn't have been the first member of the Bowen family to pull on the famous Claret and Blue. Former West Ham manager Harry Redknapp tried to sign his father, Sam, from Southern League club Merthyr Tydfil way back in August 1996 — four months before Jarrod was born!

STAT ATTACK!
2019/20:
13 Premier League appearances
1 goal | **4** assists
1.8 shots per game (on average)
155 recoveries
17 goals in **32** Championship games for Hull City

PREMIER LEAGUE CAREER:
20 appearances
27 shots
283 passes
21 tackles

CAREER HISTORY:
Hereford United (2013-2014)
Hull City (2014-2020)
West Ham United (2020-present)

*Stats correct as of end of 2019/20 Premier League season

IRONS INSIDER: MICHAIL ANTONIO!

A huge character, a hard worker and a history-making Hammer – Michail Antonio is a modern-day West Ham United icon!

FULL NAME:
Michail Gregory Antonio

BORN:
28 March 1990

PLACE OF BIRTH:
Wandsworth, England

NICKNAME:
'Mick' or 'The Beast'!

After starting his career at non-League club Tooting & Mitcham United, Antonio worked his way up the Football League ladder via spells at the likes of Reading, Southampton, Sheffield Wednesday and Nottingham Forest.

Along with his friendly and funny character, Antonio's will to win is second-to-none, and saw him shine upon signing for West Ham United in September 2015; few players can cover as much ground, or fulfil as many roles, as the Irons' No30.

A supreme athlete, Antonio possesses pace, power, persistence and – as he showed so successfully last season – a predatory instinct in front of goal.

He had the best season of his career to date in 2019/20, scoring eight times as a striker in the final month of the campaign to win Premier League Player of the Month and seal our safety. During that time, he became the first West Ham player ever to score four goals in a Premier League game, putting Norwich City to the sword at Carrow Road!

The signs are he's just going to keep getting better – so look out for more of Mick's interesting goal celebrations in the years ahead!

WHAT THEY SAY ABOUT HIM:

"Michail has been really, really important to us. He's played great and he has matured a lot recently. He's looking after himself in a way that gives him every chance of performing well and all those things are helping him. Mick's certainly stepped up to the plate. I'm really pleased for him." DAVID MOYES

STAT ATTACK!
2019/20:
13 Premier League appearances
10 goals
(2 headers, 7 right-footed, 1 left-footed)
68 shots
3 assists

PREMIER LEAGUE CAREER:

133 appearances
36 goals
298 shots (**114** on target)
14 assists

INSIDER FACT:
During the lockdown period last year, Antonio's wife was pregnant, so the ever-adaptable father-of-four had to fulfil yet another role – home-schooling all his kids! "They liked PE, obviously, but didn't like English because of the comprehension and stuff you have to deal with! It brought memories back!" Antonio laughed.

CAREER HISTORY:
Tooting & Mitcham United (2007-2008)
Reading (2008-2012, including loans)
Sheffield Wednesday (2012-2014)
Nottingham Forest (2014-2015)
West Ham United (2015-present)

*Stats correct as of end of 2019/20 Premier League season

41

10 THINGS
YOU DIDN'T KNOW ABOUT
DAVID MOYES!

David William Moyes is one of the hardest-working and most experienced and passionate managers in the Premier League, and he brings those qualities into every single West Ham United game he manages.

Reappointed for a second spell with the Hammers on 29 December 2019, how much do you really know about the gaffer? Make sure you get clued up right here!

1 Moyes has been in charge for more Premier League matches than any other currently-serving manager – only Sir Alex Ferguson, Arsene Wenger and Harry Redknapp have overseen more games!

2 During those games, Moyes has seen his sides rack up over 200 top-flight wins, accumulate over 750 points and score over 700 goals!

3 In terms of personal accolades, Moyes has been named Premier League Manager of the Month on TEN occasions throughout his career, and has been named the League Managers' Association Manager of the Year a further THREE times!

4 Despite being born in Glasgow, Moyes actually started his youth career as a defender with IBV, the second-oldest club in Iceland! He was scouted through a family friend.

5 Moyes made over 550 appearances as a tough-tackling centre-back, enjoying the most success as a player at boyhood club Celtic, where he won the Scottish Premier Division title.

6 Always a student of the beautiful game, Moyes took his first coaching badges at just 22 years of age, while also compiling notes on the coaching techniques of all the different managers he had played under!

7 In his first job as a manager, the Glaswegian took just two seasons to get Preston North End promoted once, before narrowly missing out on a second promotion – to the Premier League – the season after!

8 At Everton, Moyes helped the Toffees secure their highest-ever Premier League finish – fourth in 2004/05 – qualify for the UEFA Champions League, reach an FA Cup Final and achieve no fewer than five top-six finishes! These remarkable achievements led to his move to Manchester United.

9 Ever diligent and keen to help others, Moyes volunteered during the initial stages of the coronavirus pandemic, delivering baskets of healthy food in the Lancashire village where he lives with his wife Pamela.

10 Moyes is never prepared to settle for anything less than 100% commitment – and ambition – from his players. "I always want to finish at the top, I always want to be first," he told the media recently. "I'm not starting the season to finish just outside the bottom three. We'll start the season looking to win every game."

"What we need is the players to buy into everything we want. I want to give the crowd something to shout about and cheer about. I am a football supporter and always have been and I know what the supporters want – they want to see action and they want to see commitment from the players. So, what I will guarantee is that me and the staff will try and get every drop out of the players that we can and hopefully, in turn, it will get us further up the league. Then, I really want to try and build something that looks good for the future."

DAVID MOYES

EYE ON THE BALL!

Everybody knows in football it's always important to keep your eye on the ball... but in the case of these six pictures from last season, we've no idea which one!

Two of the balls in each picture are fake – but can you tell which one's real in each of the cases below?

1

A B C

ANSWER C

1895

1
YE
TOGI

WEST H

1895 12

2

A B C

ANSWER B

betway

3

A B C

ANSWER C

5 2020

RS
THER

4

ANSWER

A   B   C

A

B

C

5

ANSWER

3

ANSWER

A

B

C

6

10 FASCINATING FACTS ABOUT
LONDON STADIUM

2020/21 will be West Ham United's FIFTH season in their ultra-swanky home in Queen Elizabeth Olympic Park, Stratford — but how many of these fascinating facts did you know about London Stadium?

1 Our first-ever match at London Stadium came in the Europa League qualifying rounds on 4 August 2016. Slovenian side NK Domzale were the opposition — and the Hammers swiftly set about crowning their new home in style, beating them 3-0!

2 Cheikhou Kouyate grabbed our first-ever goal at the ground that day! The Senegalese midfielder burst into the box and, when defender Sam Byram mis-hit his shot, Kouyate reacted instinctively to flick the ball low past the Domzale keeper. He later grabbed another, before Sofiane Feghouli rounded off the scoring for the Irons.

3 London Stadium played host to the 2012 Olympic and Paralympic Games, where Team GB wowed the world by winning an astonishing 185 medals in total — 65 medals (29 gold, 17 silver and 19 bronze) for the Olympians, and 120 (34 gold, 43 silver and 43 bronze) for the Paralympians!

4 The Stadium was built over three years, with construction work beginning in spring 2008. During that time, 800,000 tonnes of soil were removed to make way for the foundations — just for context, that's the weight of... ooh... 61,000 double-decker buses!

5 While football is where the action is mainly at, London Stadium has also hosted many other events in its time. From the 2017 World Athletics and World Para Athletics Championships, to the Anniversary Games, the Great Newham Run, the 2015 Rugby World Cup, and musical concerts from the likes of the Rolling Stones, Guns N' Roses, Jay-Z, Beyonce, Robbie Williams – and scheduled for 2021, Green Day – there's a wide variety of sights and sounds to be enjoyed in Stratford!

6 As of August 2020, the Stadium has a massive matchday capacity of 60,000 when operating in football mode – but it can fit up to 80,000 for concerts and other events! Those numbers include 428 wheelchair viewing spaces, 3600 people in hospitality lounges and executive boxes – and, from 2020, a new fully-equipped Sensory Room, where fans with sensory difficulties can still enjoy the match!

7 Three of the stands in the Hammers' majestic home are named after Club legends: the influential Bobby Moore, the legendary midfielder Sir Trevor Brooking and, as of March 2019, our all-time appearance record holder, Billy Bonds!

8 The Claret and Blue Army will be closer to the action than ever before at London Stadium during 2020/21 - two new lower tier stands behind the goals will be squared-off in line with a more traditional configuration, moving seats forward by as much as four metres!

9 West Ham United women played a historic first-ever Barclays FA Women's Super League match at the ground in September 2019 – and although they lost 2-0 on the day, it was still the Hammers' largest attendance in Women's Super League history (24,790)!

10 It is the perfect place to grab all your official West Ham United kits, collectables and merchandise – the Official Club store at London Stadium is three times bigger than its predecessor at Boleyn Ground! And, at special events, sometimes you might even meet a West Ham United player or two hanging around - decent!

THE ACADEMY OF FOOTBALL: YOUNG CHAMPIONS!

If you thought West Ham United didn't win anything in 2019/20, you should think again!

A product of one of the top football Academies in the country, West Ham Under-23s went a whole league season unbeaten under their new lead coach Dmitri Halajko, winning Premier League 2 Division 2 and scoring bucketloads of goals along the way!

Premier League 2 – Division 2

Position	Clubs	Played	Previous Points Total	Overall Points Total
1st	West Ham United	18	46	56.2
2nd	Manchester United	17	43	55.6
3rd	West Bromwich Albion	16	34	46.8
4th	Stoke City	18	27	33.0

U18 Premier League - South

Position	Clubs	Played	Previous Points Total	Overall Points Total
1st	Fulham	17	40	51.8
2nd	Chelsea	16	36	49.5
3rd	West Ham United	17	37	47.9
4th	Tottenham Hotspur	17	26	33.6

UNDER-23S: CHAMPIONS!

An unbeaten league campaign (18 games without defeat), 58 goals in that time, and the Premier League 2 Division 2 trophy – the Under-23s could hardly have had a stronger season!

Although the fixture list ultimately couldn't be completed due to the pandemic, the young Hammers were rightfully awarded their medals on a points-per-game basis, finishing ahead of title rivals Manchester United and securing promotion to the top league for 2020/21.

On top of that, the Under-23s also reached the semi-finals of the Premier League International Cup, knocking out top-tier sides like Brighton & Hove Albion and Derby County! Sadly, though, the tournament could not be completed – so they'll just have to do the same next year!

UNDER-18S PUSH RIVALS ALL THE WAY!

The Under-18s, under former Hammer Kevin Keen, also enjoyed a brilliant season, pushing London rivals Fulham and Chelsea all the way in the U18 Premier League title race!

The youth team were particularly lethal in front of goal once again, scoring 51 times in 17 matches – that's an average of three goals every game!

Despite being on a great run of form, the global pandemic halted their 2019/20 campaign, with West Ham finishing third on a points-per-game system – but if they can take that momentum into next season, they're certain to achieve big things again!

FIRST-TEAM AND FOOTBALL LEAGUE DEBUTS GALORE!

Academy football is all about challenging the young players to reach the next level – and they certainly did that!

Last season saw Premier League debuts for winger Nathan Holland and defender Jeremy Ngakia, as well as defender Ben Johnson making an impact in the latter stages of the season.

There were Football League debuts on loan for defender Aji Alese, midfielder Conor Coventry and forwards Dan Kemp and Holland.

At international level, goalkeepers Daniel Jinadu and Krisztian Hegyi represented their nations at the

FIFA Under-17 World Cup finals, and there were loads of youth international debuts throughout the Academy ranks as the West Ham stars of the future got their names out there.

Progression, once more, was the name of the game!

AWARD WINNERS!

There were plenty of Hammers who enjoyed outstanding 2020/21 seasons, but these two scooped the Academy of Football's top individual accolades!

YOUNG HAMMER OF THE YEAR

Nathan Holland
Position: Winger (LW/RW)
D.O.B.: 19 June 1998

A goalscoring winger who loves bamboozling defenders with his quick feet and direct running, Nathan Holland was named Young Hammer of the Year 2019/20 after a breakthrough campaign.

Not only did he make his first West Ham start against Oxford United and then his Premier League debut against Wolves, Holland also registered 14 goals and eight assists in just 18 games for the Under-23s, earning a national nomination for Premier League 2 Player of the Season.

Holland then went out on loan to Oxford for the second half of the season, where he made his Football League debut and recorded an additional three goals in 12 senior appearances.

Now, he'll be looking to make a similar impression with David Moyes' Hammers at first-team level.

DYLAN TOMBIDES AWARD

Will Greenidge
Position: Defender (RB/LB)
D.O.B.: 15 May 2002

Versatile full-back Will Greenidge won the 2019/20 Dylan Tombides Award – given to the outstanding Academy scholar (Under-18s player) – after an incredibly consistent campaign.

The defender missed just one game all season for the Under-18s and recorded two assists during that time, form which was richly rewarded when he signed his first professional contract as a footballer.

Greenidge also enjoyed his first taste of senior football, starting for the Under-21s in their spectacular 5-4 win over Newport County in the EFL Trophy.

He'll now be hoping to make just as big an impact for the Under-23s this season!

For all the latest news, highlights – and of course, goals! – from the Academy of Football, be sure to follow their season on

whufc.com

RATE THE CELEBRATION!

1

9/10

2 The Classic Knee Slide

Hammers in Arms

4/10

3 Pure Passion

7/10

4 Saluting the Goal

65/10

5 Beast Mode Activated

10/10

6 Seb Delivers

1/10

5/10

7 Jarrod Jumps For Joy

9 Soucek Nearly Reaches the Sky

7.7/10

8 Sealed With a Kiss

8/10

SKILLS SCHOOL
HOW TO STAY SHARP AT HOME!

"PRACTISE, PRACTISE, PRACTISE!"

Sure, it sounds like a cliché — but every Premier League footballer will tell you one thing: they got there through putting in the hard work!

It's great to be out kicking a ball around with all your mates in the playground or the park, but there are plenty of simple games that can keep your skills sharp at home, too!

Inspired by our 'Hammers At Home' activities, here are just four easy-to-play — but difficult to master — examples.

PRACTISE YOUR FIRST-TIME PASSING!

Okay, so this one is a bit old-school. But it's a classic for a reason — every pro footy player needs two good feet to succeed!

All you need to do is find a ball, a wall, and a suitable spot where you can move backwards and forwards slightly — a few metres' distance is plenty!

Firstly, pass the ball against the wall once with your right foot. Then, when it bounces back, pass it once against the wall with your left foot.

Then do the same with your right foot — but twice — and then the same with your left foot, but twice. Keep going — three passes per foot, four passes per foot, and so on — until you reach as many passes as you can play on both your right and left foot.

Practise this one every day, and you'll be amazed how much better you'll be on your weaker foot!

THE INSIDE FOOT CHALLENGE!

This one can get pretty tiring, but it's great for working on your agility, your footwork and your ball control!

Grab yourself a ball, a stopwatch and a small patch of grass. Then, the game is simple: take as many inside foot touches as you can in the space of 45 seconds!

To get the highest score possible,

you'll want to be constantly passing the ball between your inside right and your inside left foot. It'll take a while to get the hang of it, but it will eventually almost look like you're running on the spot.

Make sure you count the touches as you go along, and keep working to up your score! For reference, one West Ham coach managed a whopping 100 — but we reckon you can beat them!

LEARN TO CONTROL ANY BOUNCE!

Another one for those of you with a ball and a wall — but this time, it's all about keeping your eye on the ball and honing your touch.

Firstly, stand maybe a metre or so away from the wall — make sure there are no windows nearby! Then, throw the ball at the wall — make sure that it's quite high, so it starts to fall down just in front of your feet after it bounces off the wall.

Don't let it land! Instead, try and take one touch and then catch it. If you manage to master that, try taking two touches before catching it.

Keep adding to the number of touches you have to take to control each bounce, and you'll soon find it easy to bring any ball down from the air — Sebastien Haller-style!

Our coach's best score was 7 touches, but there's no pressure to get close to that score straight away. Just keep trying to set yourself targets and strive to be the best you can be!

TUNE UP YOUR TEAMWORK WITH ARM TENNIS!

Okay, so you'll need a member of your household to play this one with — your brother, sister, Mum, Dad, or anyone else you live with — as well a ball that bounces and a hard floor.

Stand opposite your partner and hold opposite hands — left hand to left hand or right hand to right hand. That link will form your 'net'. (If you're slightly different heights, the taller one of you might need to kneel down!)

Then, bounce the ball on one side, and use the palm of your other hand to hit it over. Your partner should allow it to bounce once, then use the palm of their hand to return the ball over the net.

How long a rally can you and your Arm Tennis partner form? If you want to make it even more difficult, try switching to your weaker hand — or even disallowing bounces altogether!

This one's great for working on your concentration, hand-eye co-ordination — and, of course, being a team player.

WEST HAM WOMEN
THE NEXT CHAPTER!

After the thrill of an FA Cup Final and a strong first season in England's top league in 2018/19, West Ham United women's team continued to build on their massive potential last season – and an exciting new season awaits!

2019/20 SEASON REVIEW

The 2019/20 season ended in slightly unusual circumstances – with the decision made to cut short the Barclays FA Women's Super League as a result of the global pandemic – but it was still a campaign for the Irons to celebrate.

The year showed plenty of moments of quality, such as an unforgettable last-minute win over Manchester United and a 4-2 victory against Liverpool in what ended up being the final game of the season.

Ultimately, the Hammers finished eighth in the league on a points-per-game basis at the end of their second full campaign as a professional outfit.

This move gives the squad access to one of the most modern and advanced facilities in the women's top division, including 4,000 square feet of state-of-the-art pitches, a full-size indoor pitch, and innovatory medical, fitness, analysis and education facilities!

NEW MATCHDAY HOME!

Further good news followed over the summer, as the team confirmed a new matchday home from 2020/21 in the form of Dagenham & Redbridge's Victoria Road.

The move enables attendances to increase further and presents even more supporters with the exciting opportunity to watch the team and cheer on the Irons as they go for glory on the pitch!

NEW TRAINING HEADQUARTERS!

Heading into 2020/21, the team's third season in the Barclays FA WSL, and under the guidance of head coach Matt Beard, the Irons moved to a new, state-of-the-art training headquarters at Chadwell Heath, where they now train alongside the men's Academy.

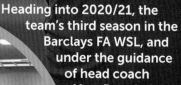

NEW FACES!

Meet some of the Hammers' new signings for the 2020/21 season!

Mackenzie Arnold

Australian international goalkeeper Mackenzie Arnold became the Irons' first new signing ahead of the new campaign when she joined from W-League side Brisbane Roar.

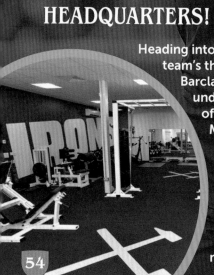

Mackenzie Arnold

Arnold is a three-time winner of the W-League Goalkeeper of the Year Award and, at international level, won the 2017 Tournament of Nations and the 2019 Cup of Nations with the Matildas.

With 188 goals in 177 games for her old side, the attacking-midfielder is considered one of Europe's leading talents, having helped Slavia Prague to five league titles and two Czech Cups.

Nor Mustafa

Young forward Nor Mustafa made the transfer to West Ham from Eskilstuna United, having come through the side's academy.

Mustafa featured in the Eskilstuna first team in the 2018/19 and 2019/20 campaigns and has also represented the Swedish national team at youth level.

Maz Pacheco

Defender Maz Pacheco made the switch to West Ham United from fellow Barclays FA WSL side Reading.

The left-back was given her professional debut by Hammers head coach Matt Beard at Liverpool and helped Doncaster Belles to win FA WSL 2 in 2018. The full-back has also represented England at U21s level.

Maz Pacheco

Nor Mustafa

Ruby Grant

Kateřina Svitková

Three-time Czech Republic Footballer of the Year Kateřina Svitková switched to east London after seven years with Slavia Prague.

Ruby Grant

Ruby Grant made the move to the Irons on a short-term deal, after the pandemic postponed the midfielder's plan to head to university in the United States of America.

A graduate of the Arsenal Academy, Grant notably scored a hat-trick for the Gunners in a 4-0 win over Crawley Town in the 2018/19 FA Cup.

Kateřina Svitková

Hawa Cissoko

Hawa Cissoko

Versatile defender Hawa Cissoko joined West Ham United from ASJ Soyaux.

The French international has previously played for Paris Saint-Germain and Marseille, and made her debut for the national team in a 3-1 win over Spain in September 2017.

CAN YOU WIN THE PREMIER LEAGUE?

Listen up, because this is your chance to win the greatest prize in English football: the Premier League trophy!

Over the next few pages, you'll find 38 multiple-choice questions about West Ham United – one for every Premier League game they'll play in 2020/21.

If you answer a question correctly, mark that game as a 'Win' and award yourself **3** points!

If you're stuck, you can move on to the next question – put that down as a 'Draw' and award yourself **1** point. **WARNING:** You can only have five draws in the entire quiz!

If you get one wrong, it's a 'Loss' – it's **0** points for that question, but keep your head up and keep going!

See how many points you can get over the course of the season – and then check the table to see if it's enough to get that Premier League trophy dressed in Claret and Blue! Come on you Irons!

WEST HAM UNITED FOOTBALL CLUB

1 West Ham United were originally founded in 1895 under what name?

a) Thames Ironworks FC;
b) East London Hammers;
c) Claret Rangers

ANSWER: C

2 At which stadium do West Ham play their home matches?

a) Wembley Stadium;
b) Old Trafford;
c) London Stadium

ANSWER: C

3 What is the name of the West Ham United mascot?

a) Hammerhead;
b) Hammertongs;
c) Hammerman

ANSWER: a

4 What was the first trophy West Ham ever won, way back in 1958?

a) FA Cup; b) League Cup;
c) Second Division

ANSWER: C

5 With 326 strikes, who is West Ham's all-time top goalscorer?

a) Geoff Hurst; b) Vic Watson;
c) Jimmy Ruffell

ANSWER: b

6 West Ham left Boleyn Ground in 2016; who scored the last-ever goal there?

a) Diafra Sakho;
b) Michail Antonio;
c) Winston Reid

ANSWER: b

7 How many goals did West Ham United score in all competitions in 2019/20?

a) 44; b) 49; c) 53

ANSWER: b

8 Delays made 2019/20 our longest-ever season – how many days did it last?

a) 322; b) 351; c) 364

ANSWER: A

9 Which Hammer has made the most West Ham appearances in history (799)?

a) Billy Bonds;
b) Bobby Moore;
c) Trevor Brooking

ANSWER: a

10 Which of these Hammers was NOT in their country's squad at the last European Championships in 2016?

a) Angelo Ogbonna;
b) Issa Diop;
c) Darren Randolph

ANSWER: C

11 Who is the youngest player from these 2019/20 signings?

a) Pablo Fornals;
b) Tomas Soucek;
c) Jarrod Bowen

ANSWER: C

56

1895   125 YEARS   2020

12 Who wears the Number 16 shirt for West Ham?

a) Mark Noble;
b) Aaron Cresswell;
c) Robert Snodgrass

ANSWER: _____A_____

13 Sebastien Haller was signed from which German club in 2019?

a) Bayern Munich;
b) VfL Wolfsburg;
c) Eintracht Frankfurt

ANSWER: _____b_____

14 Who was the most recent West Ham United manager before David Moyes?

a) Gianfranco Zola;
b) Sam Allardyce;
c) Manuel Pellegrini

ANSWER: _____C_____

15 Which of these Hammers is NOT an Academy of Football graduate?

a) Aaron Cresswell;
b) Mark Noble;
c) Ben Johnson

ANSWER: _____C_____

16 How many goals did Michail Antonio score in total last season?

a) 8; b) 10; c) 12

ANSWER: _____a_____

17 Who scored West Ham's first-ever goal at London Stadium (in August 2016)?

a) Diafra Sakho;
b) Michail Antonio;
c) Cheikhou Kouyate

ANSWER: _____

18 Who was the first professional female football player in West Ham United history (signing in 2018)?

a) Martha Thomas;
b) Vyan Sampson;
c) Rosie Kmita

ANSWER: _____

19 Who is West Ham's all-time youngest player?

a) Reece Oxford;
b) Ben Johnson;
c) Freddie Sears

ANSWER: _____

20 Which midfielder won the Hammer of the Year award in 2019/20?

a) Mark Noble;
b) Tomas Soucek;
c) Declan Rice

ANSWER: _____

21 And who was named Young Hammer of the Year?

a) Nathan Holland;
b) Conor Coventry;
c) Grady Diangana

ANSWER: _____

22 Which League One side did West Ham beat in the FA Cup third round last season?

a) Ipswich Town;
b) Gillingham;
c) Lincoln City

ANSWER: _____

23 Up until 2016, where did West Ham United's first team train?

a) Rush Green; b) Stratford;
c) Chadwell Heath

ANSWER: _____

24 Who scored West Ham's most recent goal in the Europe (against Astra Giurgiu in August 2016)?

a) Mark Noble;
b) Diafra Sakho;
c) Javier 'Chicharito' Hernandez

ANSWER: _____

25 Who were the opponents for David Moyes' first game of his second spell in charge of the Club?

a) Sheffield United;
b) Liverpool;
c) Bournemouth

ANSWER: _____

26 Which player scored a last-gasp winner in the 3-2 win over Chelsea in July 2020?

a) Tomas Soucek;
b) Andriy Yarmolenko;
c) Michail Antonio

ANSWER: _____

27 How many times have West Ham United won the FA Cup in their history?

a) 2; b) 3; c) 4

ANSWER: _____

28 Which of these shirt numbers has West Ham retired?

a) 6; b) 14; c) 20

ANSWER: _____

29 In what month does Mark Noble celebrate his birthday?

a) May; b) August;
c) September

ANSWER: _____

30 Which Hammer famously scored a World Cup Final hat-trick in 1966?

a) Martin Peters;
b) Bobby Moore;
c) Geoff Hurst

ANSWER: _____

31 Which Italian giants featured in London Stadium's official opening game in August 2016?

a) AC Milan;
b) Juventus;
c) AS Roma

ANSWER: _____

32 Who was the last West Ham United player to score a winning goal in a Championship Play-Off Final?

a) Ricardo Vaz Te;
b) Carlton Cole;
c) Bobby Zamora

ANSWER: _____

33 Which one of these former Hammers is their country's all-time leading goalscorer?

a) Modibo Maiga;
b) Enner Valencia;
c) Javier 'Chicharito' Hernandez

ANSWER: _____

34 Sebastien Haller won more aerial challenges than any other Premier League player last season – with how many successes?

a) 184; b) 218; c) 249

ANSWER: _____

35 Which Premier League team did Michail Antonio score four goals against in July 2020?

a) Norwich City;
b) Watford;
c) Brighton & Hove Albion

ANSWER: _____

36 Who captained West Ham United women during most of 2019/20?

a) Kate Longhurst;
b) Adriana Leon;
c) Gilly Flaherty

ANSWER: _____

37 Which of these three teams did West Ham NOT win both league games against last season?

a) Chelsea;
b) Southampton;
c) Bournemouth

ANSWER: _____

38 West Ham are one of only how many teams never to have fallen below the second division of English football?

a) Four; b) Six; c) Eight

ANSWER: _____

POINTS TOTAL	RESULT
95 or more	Premier League Champions! You did it – you've just won West Ham United their first-ever top-flight title! You're a Claret and Blue hero!
85 – 94	Runners-up! Fantastic effort! You were just pipped to the title this year, but a silver medal for the season is still magnificent!
70 – 84	Champions League qualification! Nice – you're in the top four, and will be playing in Europe's premier club competition next season!
60 – 69	Europa League! Not bad at all – we'll see you jet-setting around Europe next season!
46 – 59	Mid-table! Not bad, but we know you can achieve bigger things!
36 – 45	Survival! You've rescued your Premier League place for the next campaign.
35 or below	Relegation! Don't be discouraged, though – try again! We know you'll do better next time.

DID YOU KNOW?:

The Hammers' highest-ever Premier League points tally was 62, in 2015/16, when they finished seventh under Croatian manager Slaven Bilic.

Their highest-ever Premier League finish, meanwhile, came back in 1998/99, when the Irons ended the season in fifth place!

58

ANSWERS ON PAGES 60-61

COLOUR IN CHALLENGE!

No pressure... but our captain, **Mark Noble**, is counting on you!

Somebody's come along and stolen all the colours from this picture of our skipper. To sort things out, you'll need to get out your colouring pencils or crayons – and show off those artistic skills!

Make sure you pick the right colours for his shirt, socks and boots. Stay within the lines, and, if you're particularly up for a challenge, see if you can colour the background in correctly, too! Good luck!

PUZZLE SOLUTIONS

PAGES 24-25. WHO'S BEHIND THE FILTERS?

1. Michail Antonio

2. Aaron Cresswell

3. Issa Diop

4. Darren Randolph

5. Robert Snodgrass

6. Kate Longhurst

7. Andriy Yarmolenko & Declan Rice

8. Ben Johnson

9. Gilly Flaherty

10. David Martin

PAGE 30. 50/50S:

Michail Antonio
Declan Rice
Vic Watson
Hammerhead
17
The Cockney Rejects
1964
Aaron Cresswell

ANAGRAMS:

DECLAN RICE
MARK NOBLE
MOORE
ISSA DIOP
DI CANIO
TOMAS SOUCEK
GEOFF HURST

PAGE 31. WORDSEARCH:

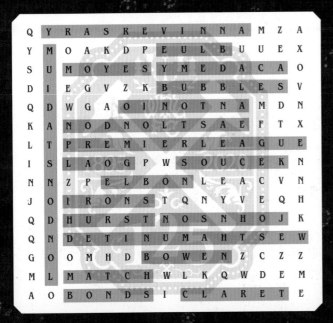

```
Q  Y R A S R E V I N N A M Z A
Y  M O A K D P E U L B U U E X
S  U M O Y E S Y M E D A C A O
D  I E G V Z K B U B B L E S V
Q  D W G A O I N O T N A M D N
K  A N O D N O L T S A E F T X
L  T P R E M I E R L E A G U E
I  S L A O G P W S O U C E K N
N  N Z P E L B O N L E A C V N
J  O I R O N S T Q N Y V E Q H
Q  D H U R S T N O S N H O J K
Q  N D E T I N U M A H T S E W
G  O O M H D B O W E N Z C Z Z
M  L M A T C H W L K Q W D E M
A  O B O N D S I C L A R E T E
```

PAGES 38-39. SPOT THE DIFFERENCE

1. Fredericks' heart logo disappears from shirt
2. Diop's right sock loses its logo
3. Letter 'P' is missing from 'Pretty Bubbles in the air' on seat cover in background
4. Logo is missing from Ogbonna's right sleeve
5. Sock stripe is missing from Rice's right sock
6. Yellow panel is missing from linesman's flag in background
7. The colour of Fredericks' boots changes
8. Fredericks' short number changes from 24 to 23
9. Stripe at the bottom of Diop's shorts is Blue instead of Claret
10. Ball added to the side of the pitch in the background

PAGES 44-45. EYE ON THE BALL!

1. A
2. B
3. C
4. B
5. A
6. C

PAGES 56-58. CAN YOU WIN THE PREMIER LEAGUE?

1 a	9 a	17 c	25 c	33 c
2 c	10 b	18 c	26 b	34 b
3 a	11 c	19 a	27 b	35 a
4 c	12 a	20 c	28 a	36 c
5 b	13 c	21 a	29 a	37 c
6 c	14 c	22 b	30 c	38 c
7 c	15 a	23 c	31 b	
8 b	16 b	24 a	32 a	

DO YOU KNOW THE WORDS TO

I'M FOREVER BLOWING BUBBLES?

FILL IN THE BLANKS!